PUBLISHING

Healthy Eating, Healthy Living!

Book 3

Helping children to achieve a healthy balance in their lives

Years 5 & 6

Judith Drysdale

Title: Healthy Eating, Healthy Living Book 3: Years 5 & 6

Author: Judith Drysdale

Designer: Delineate Ltd

Editor: Tanya Tremewan

Book code: PB00115

ISBN: 978-1-908735-94-2

Published: 2012

Publisher: TTS Group Ltd

Park Lane Business Park
Kirkby-in-Ashfield
Notts, NG17 9GU
Tel: 0800 318 686
Fax: 0800 137 525

Website: www.tts-shopping.com

About the author: Having taught extensively in New Zealand and Australia, Judith Drysdale has now settled in the warm and sunny Hervey Bay, Queensland where she writes full time for children aged 5 to 11 years. Her long-time interest and involvement in health, coupled with her concern over the rise in child obesity and type 2 diabetes, fostered her desire to influence children's attitudes to good health and wise food choices.

CONTENTS

INTRODUCTION

In this *Healthy Eating, Healthy Living* series you have a range of convenient tools for informing children of the nutritional needs of their bodies in an accessible, meaningful way. Providing this information is clearly urgent. In 2006 nearly 30% of children aged 2 to 15 years in the UK were classified as overweight or obese.[1] Type 2 diabetes is also prevalent in our societies and, although it has long been regarded as a disease of adulthood, is being found increasingly among children and young people.[2]

In this context, it is essential for schools to play their part in empowering children to make informed decisions about what they eat – and about what they do as well. To make a difference, we must incorporate good diet and exercise into children's daily routine. A school will be more successful in this task if it works in partnership with children's families. This resource helps to build this partnership through activities to be done at home, increasing awareness among parents and carers of what their children are learning at school and providing them with the opportunity to address weight concerns related to the youngest generation.

Together the three books in this series cover Key Stages 1 and 2. All follow the same structure and could be used concurrently in different classes. At all levels, the activities help to create the momentum needed for changing one's lifestyle and managing weight. This book for Upper Key Stage 2 builds on the nutritional knowledge they gained in Book 2. It introduces the concept of food groups, linking it closely to pupils' own experiences of food. It also encourages learning through an investigative approach. There are surveys to find out about the lifestyles of friends and family, as well as a research booklet with which pupils learn more about vitamins, minerals and body structures. Pupils may do their research individually or in small groups and then form conclusions about the data they collect.

By using this resource, you will cover the National Curriculum learning objectives outlined in the chart on the following page.

Note: The author of this book offers these lifestyle suggestions based on widely available, evidence-based advice. However, Essential Resources emphasises that individuals differ in their nutritional and exercise requirements and takes no responsibility for the consequences of following the suggestions in this book.

---

1. UK Department of Health website: <www.dh.gov.uk>.
2. A Fagot-Campagna, K M Venkat Narayan and G Imperatore (2001) Editorial: Type 2 diabetes in children. *British Medical Journal* 322: 377–378. Available online at: <bmj.bmjjournals.com>.

CURRICULUM LINKS

Key Stage 2 (Years 5–6)

Subject	Objective(s)
Knowledge, skills and understanding	*Pupils should be taught:*
Personal, social and health education – Developing a healthy, safer lifestyle	• what makes a healthy lifestyle, including the benefits of exercise and healthy eating, and how to make informed choices
Physical education – Knowledge and understanding of fitness and health	• why physical activity is good for their health and wellbeing
Science – Life processes and living things: humans and other animals	• (nutrition) about the need for food for activity and growth, and about the importance of an adequate and varied diet for health • (health) about the importance of exercise for good health
Breadth of opportunities	*Pupils should be taught the knowledge, skills and understanding through opportunities to:*
Personal, social and health education	• make real choices and decisions (eg, about issues affecting their health and wellbeing)

Source: Adapted from National Curriculum Online <curriculum.qca.org.uk>

A. HEALTHY KIDS

What is healthy living?

Healthy living means keeping all the things in our life in balance. That is, we live in a healthy way when we have not too much of one thing and just enough of another.

1. Match these items to show they are in balance:

work, exercise, food eaten, £ earned, play, £ spent

____________________ balanced by ____________________

____________________ balanced by ____________________

____________________ balanced by ____________________

To stay healthy, your body needs to stay in **energy balance**. This means:

Energy in	–	Same energy used	=	Energy balance
Too much in	–	Not enough used	=	Overweight
Not enough in	–	Too much used	=	Overtired

2. If you put more energy (food) in to your body than the energy you burn off, what will your body do with it?

☐ Nothing ☐ Get rid of it ☐ Use it to grow fatter

3. A balanced diet with a balanced lifestyle will give you a **healthy balance**.

a. What do you think a **balanced diet** is?

____

b. List the foods that you think you should eat every day as part of a balanced diet.

____________________ ____________________

____________________ ____________________

____________________ ____________________

____________________ ____________________

____________________ ____________________

Healthy Eating, Healthy Living study

In this Healthy Eating, Healthy Living study, you will do several surveys to find out about the lifestyle and diet of your family and friends and yourself.

Here is what you will do:

- Make an attractive title page for your survey. Include your name and class, and the names of the people you surveyed.
- Use the handouts to conduct the surveys on sleep, breakfast, favourite foods, snacks, lunch and exercise. Invite 10 adults and children to take part and include them in every survey.
- Draw some conclusions from the information you have gathered. There is a handout to help you with this task too.

My planning chart

I will invite these 10 people to take part in my surveys:

1. ______________________
2. ______________________
3. ______________________
4. ______________________
5. ______________________
6. ______________________
7. ______________________
8. ______________________
9. ______________________
10. ______________________

My checklist

Tick when you have completed:

- ☐ Sleep survey
- ☐ Breakfast survey
- ☐ Favourite foods survey
- ☐ Snacks survey
- ☐ Lunch survey
- ☐ Exercise survey
- ☐ My conclusions

✓

Sleep survey

Name	How many hours do you sleep? (Write answer under the correct age group.)				
	Baby	1–4 years	5–12 years	Teen	Adult
	Amount of sleep needed				
	14–15 hours	10–13 hours	10–11 hours	8–10 hours	7–8 hours

Looking at the results ...

1. How many people get the amount of sleep they need? ____________

2. Most people get:

☐ more sleep than they need

☐ less sleep than they need

☐ the amount of sleep that they need

3. The older you get, the ______________________ sleep you need.

4. Which person in your survey gets the most sleep?

Name: ______________________________ Age: ____________

Breakfast survey

Name	Do you eat breakfast? (Answer Yes or No)	If you eat breakfast, do you eat or drink the following? (Answer Yes or No.)					
		Cereal	Toast	Yoghurt	Fruit	Milk	Other
Total							

Looking at the results ...

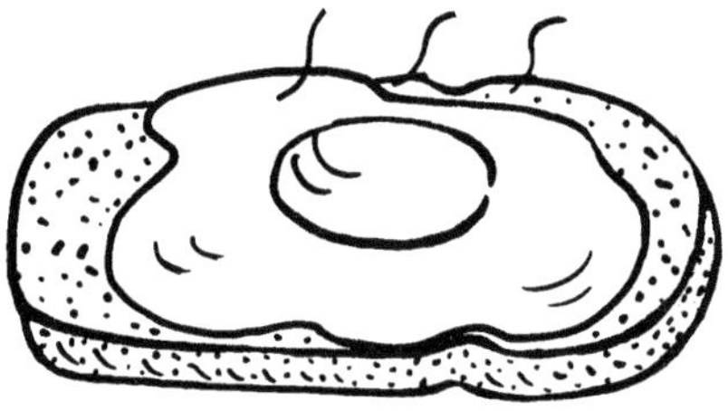

1. How many people eat breakfast?

____

2. How many people have the food and drink listed in the chart?

____

3. How many have other food and drink? ______________________

4. What is the most common breakfast of the food listed in the chart?

____

5. What do you eat for breakfast? ______________________

6. How many people in your survey eat the same breakfast as you?

____

Favourite foods survey

Name	What two groups are your favourite foods in? (Tick ✓ two groups.)						
	Grains – cereals, rice, breads, pasta, noodles	Vegetables	Fruit	Dairy – milk, yoghurt, cheese	Meat, eggs, fish, nuts, pulses	Snacks – cakes, biscuits, crisps, sweets	Takeaways
Total							

Looking at the results …

1. How many people pick takeaways as one of their favourite food groups? ______________________

2. How many people pick snacks as one of their favourite food groups? ______________________

3. How many people pick fruit or vegetables as one of their favourite food groups? ______________________

4. What are the two most popular food groups?

____

Snacks survey

Name	Adult or young person?	Do you snack on the following every day? (Answer Yes or No.)					
		Fruit	Cakes or biscuits	Pies or pastries	Sweets or chocolate	Crisps	Other
Total							

Looking at the results ...

1. What is the most common snack? ______________________

2. Is there any snack that **no** young person eats? If so, what is it?

____

3. How many people eat more than one kind of snack every day?

____

4. How many people eat fruit as a snack? ______________________

5. How many people said they had a snack every day other than the kinds listed in the survey? ______________________

Lunch survey

Name	Adult or young person?	What food groups do you eat for lunch? (Tick ✓ each one that applies.)					
		Fruit	Yoghurt, cheese, milk	Vegetables (including salad)	Breads, pasta, noodles, rice	Meat, fish, eggs, nuts	Cakes, biscuits, pies, pastries
Total							

Looking at the results ...

1. What food group is eaten by the most people? ____________________

2. How many young people eat the most popular food group?

____

3. What food group is eaten by the smallest number of people?

____

4. How many adults eat the least popular food group? ____________________

Exercise survey

Name	Adult or young person?	How long do you exercise each day? (Tick ✓ the answer.)					
		No exercise	It's not every day but I do a bit	15 minutes	½ hour	1 hour	2 hours or more
Total							

Looking at the results ...

1. What is the most common length of time for people to exercise?

____

2. Compare this most common length of time with the amount of exercise you do. Is it more, less or the same? ________________

3. How many young people exercise every day? ________________

4. How many adults exercise every day? ________________

5. How many people do no exercise? ________________

6. Who does the most exercise every day? ________________

My conclusions

1. Sleep

Most of the people I interviewed:

☐ Get enough sleep ☐ Do not get enough sleep

☐ Sleep more than they need to

Write a comment about something interesting you found in your data.

____

____

2. Breakfast

Most people I interviewed:

☐ Eat breakfast ☐ Skip breakfast

The most common breakfast is ______________________.

Write a comment about something interesting you found in your data.

____

____

3. Favourite foods

The favourite food group for adults is ______________________.

The favourite food group for young people is ______________________.

Write a comment about something interesting you found in your data.

____

____

4. Snacks

The most common snack food for adults is ______________________.

The most common snack food for young people is ______________________

Write a comment about something interesting you found in your data.

____

____

5. Lunch

Most adults eat lunch from the ______________________,

__________________ and __________________ food groups.

Most young people eat lunch from the ________________,

__________________ and __________________ food groups.

The largest number of food groups chosen by one person was

__________________.

The smallest number of food groups chosen by one person was

__________________.

Most of the people I interviewed ate a __________________

(healthy, unhealthy) lunch.

6. Exercise

/10 never exercise. /10 exercise for 1 hour or more each day.

The most common length of time for adults to exercise was

__________________.

The most common length of time for young people to exercise

was __________________.

Write a comment about something interesting you found in your data.

____

____

7. Overall

Do you think most of the people you interviewed live a healthy, balanced life?

☐ Yes ☐ No

Comment

____

____

____

B. EATING FOR HEALTH: WHAT FOODS ARE HEALTHY

Introducing the five food groups

There are five main food groups that provide your body with all the nutrients that it needs to keep you healthy.

1. Here are the five main food groups. Give six examples of foods in each group.

Vegetable

Examples:

____

____

____

____

____

____

Fruit

Examples:

____

____

____

____

____

____

Bread, cereals, rice, pasta, noodles

Examples:

(Here you might think of types of bread, cereals etc.)

____

____

____

____

Milk, cheese, yoghurt

Examples:

(Here you might think of types of milk, cheese etc.)

Meat, fish, eggs, nuts, pulses

Examples:

(Here you might think of types of meat, fish etc.)

There are extra foods that are not in the five main food groups. You should eat only small amounts of those foods.

2. Can you think of some extra foods that are not in the five main food groups? List them here.

Climb aboard the Healthy Living Spaceship

Colour your spaceship and use it as a guide to the following activities.

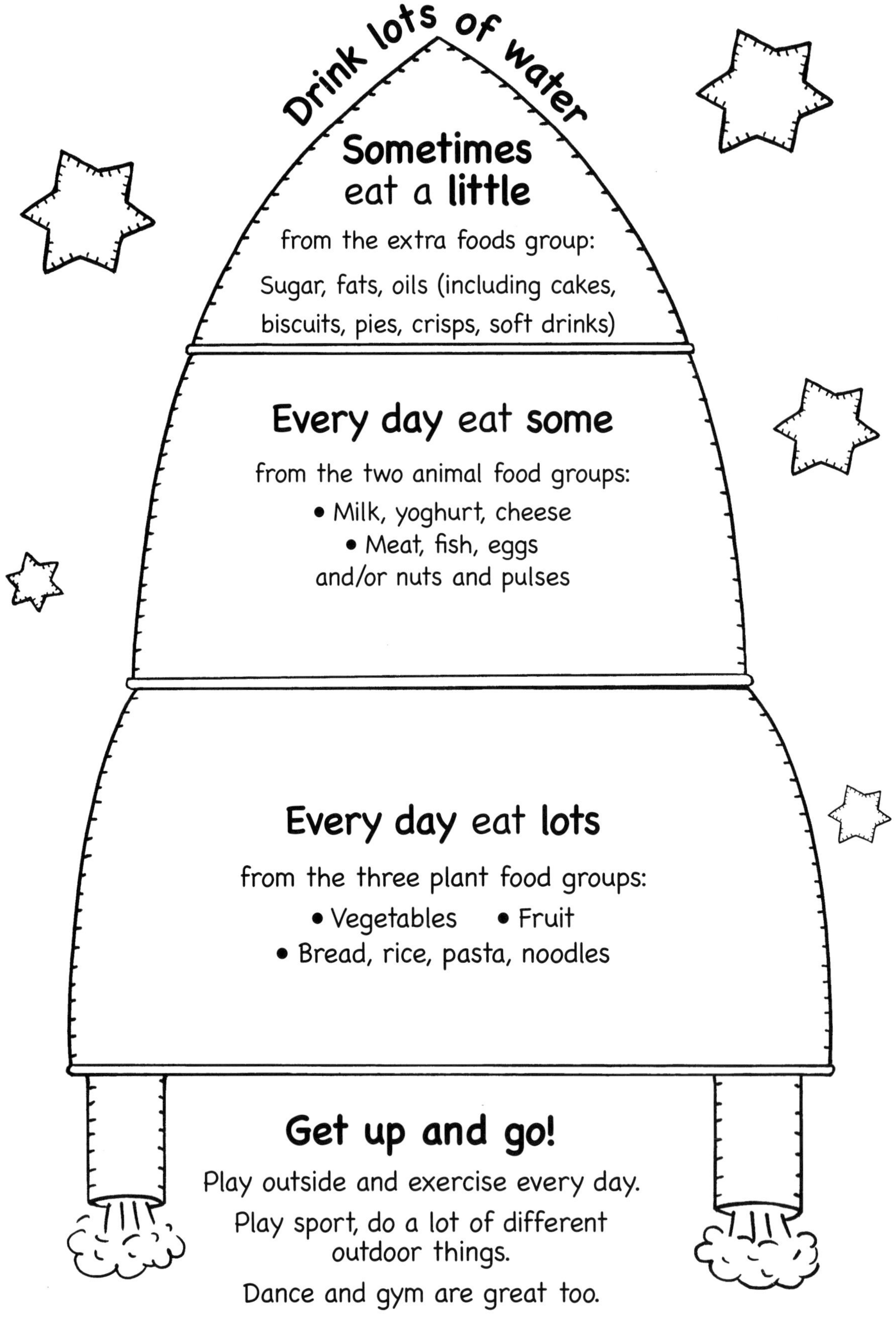

Healthy Living Spaceship challenge

Teacher note: Make an enlarged copy of the Healthy Living Spaceship from the previous page as a guide to this activity.

Make a model of the Healthy Living Spaceship.

What you need

- 1 large rectangular carton (for the base of the spaceship)

- 1 rectangular carton that is about same width as the large one but shorter (for the middle)

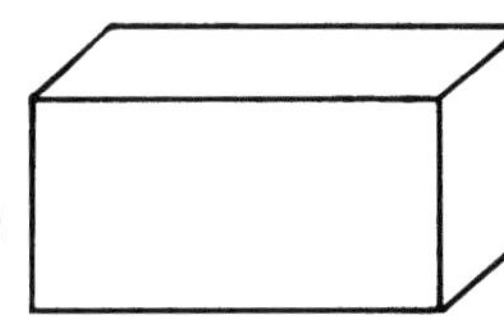

- 1 piece of flat cardboard to make a small cone (for the nose of the spaceship)

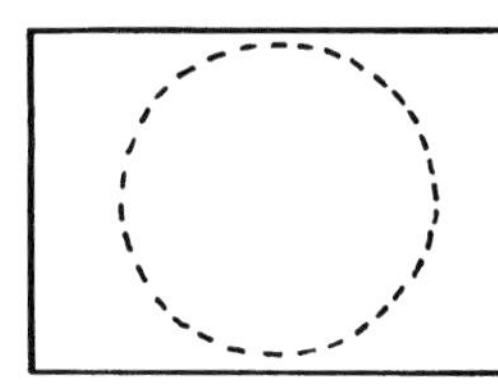

- 2 large yoghurt (or similar) pots (as "exhaust pipes" for the rocket's thrust)

- Streamers (for the energy)

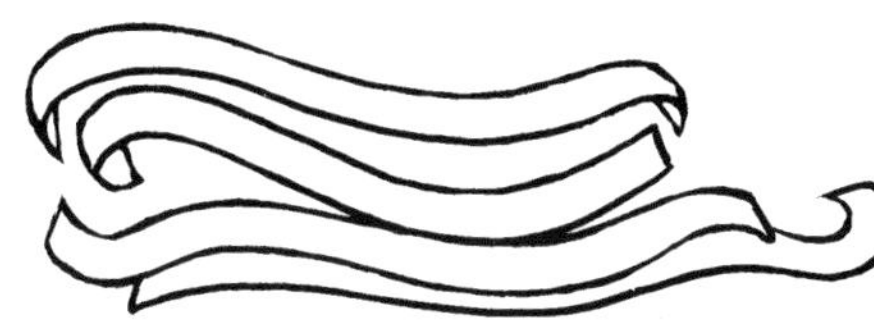

- Pictures of foods (to glue on the right parts of the spaceship)

- Glue

What to do

1. Glue the two larger rectangular cartons end to end.

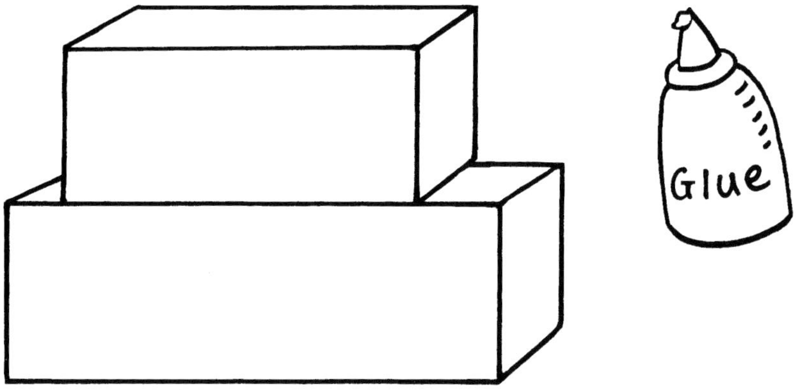

2. Cut out a circle from a piece of cardboard and use it to make a cone from a circle (see diagram). Make small cuts all round the circumference of your cone to make a flat surface for gluing. Glue it on to the top of the smaller carton.

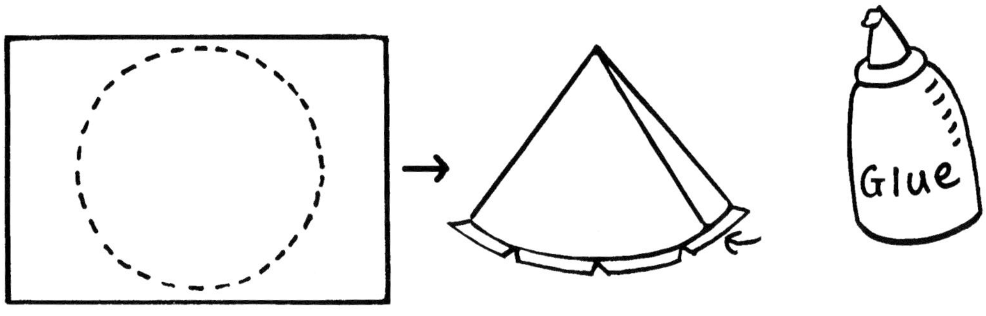

3. Glue the bottom of the pots to the underside of the rocket, one at each end.

4. Cut out food pictures from magazines and make a collage of the appropriate foods for each part of the spaceship. (Overlap the pictures so that no part of the cartons shows through.)

5. Glue the "energy" strips on to the base of the spaceship.

6. Write (or produce on computer) neat labels for each part of the Healthy Living Spaceship.

Do a library display of the Healthy Living Spaceships that you and your classmates have made. You could include your other work – such as your survey or research booklets – as part of the display.

Explore the Healthy Living Spaceship

Use your copy of the Healthy Living Spaceship to help you with this activity.

1. What is the best drink for healthy people? ____________________

2. What may we eat a **little** of **sometimes**?

   ____________ ____________ ____________

   ____________ ____________ ____________

3. What are six foods that we get from animals?

   ____________ ____________ ____________

   ____________ ____________ ____________

4. What are six foods that we get from plants?

   ____________ ____________ ____________

   ____________ ____________ ____________

5. Which food groups are the most important for our health?

   ____

6. What must we do to balance the food we eat?

   ____

7. Some people choose not to eat a food because they think they don't like it. But there are other reasons why some people do not eat certain foods shown in the spaceship. What are some of those reasons?

   ____

   ____

8. Write a sentence about what the Healthy Living Spaceship teaches you.

   ____

   ____

Start the day the breakfast way

Imagine you are a car. Every day you go on a long journey and, after a night of rest, you need to fill up your empty fuel tank before you head out on the road again. Breakfast is great fuel. Researchers have found that children who eat breakfast perform better, behave better and score higher in tests.

To be a good fuel, your breakfast should also be healthy. You need foods with:

- **carbohydrate** to give you energy
- **calcium** and **protein** to make your bones, teeth and muscles strong
- **vitamins** and **minerals** to keep your skin and body healthy.

1. From the chart below, choose a low fat, low sugar breakfast that gives you all the **nutrients** (nourishing ingredients) that your body needs to be healthy. We have put each food under the category where it fits best but some foods contain more than one of these nutrients.

Healthy breakfast menu

Carbohydrates	Calcium	Protein	Vitamins and minerals
Whole grain toast (2) Rice Cereal	Yoghurt Low fat milk or soy milk Smoothie	Peanut butter Egg Nuts	Marmite Fresh fruit Fruit juice Banana Raisins

My healthy choices from the healthy breakfast menu

2. Use the suggestions in this chart plus your own ideas to **plan a week of healthy breakfasts**. Choose at least one food from each food group for each breakfast.

One week of healthy breakfasts: my plan

	Carbohydrate Whole grain toast, rice, cereal	Calcium Yoghurt, smoothie, cheese	Protein Peanut butter, egg, nuts	Vitamins and minerals Fresh fruit, Marmite, raisins	Drinks Water, low fat milk or soy milk, juice
Monday					
Tuesday					
Wednesday					
Thursday					
Friday					

3. Now take your plan home and try it!

Fuel and energy balance

When you work or play or even sleep, your body uses energy. Your body needs fuel (food) to provide enough energy to work efficiently. But you must add the **right amount** of fuel so that it balances with the amount of energy you use.

- If you put in **too much** fuel, you have more energy than you need and the excess energy builds fat.
- If you put in **too little** fuel, you won't have enough energy so you will feel tired.

Energy in food is measured in kilojoules. Check out the "Energy" information on food packages and compare the amount of energy in various foods.

The diagram below shows how we get different kinds of energy from different kinds of nutrients.

Sources of energy

Carbohydrates

Your body uses carbohydrates for energy. They make your muscles work so you should eat some in every meal if you are active. Bread, cereals, pasta, rice, fruits and vegetables contain carbohydrates that give lasting energy.

Protein

You get the same amount of energy from protein as from carbohydrates but your body uses it for a different purpose – to help you build muscles and grow strong. Protein is found in red meat, chicken, fish, eggs, nuts, dairy foods and pulses.

Fats

Fats give you twice as much energy as carbohydrates and protein. They also provide extra padding on the body. You can get fats from butter, oil, margarine, nuts, dairy foods, meat and processed foods.

Fluid

Fluid does not give energy but your body must have it in order to use the energy foods properly. You need about six glasses of water a day to keep your body working well. You should also drink milk and unsweetened fruit juice so that you gain the other nutrients in them.

1. Use the facts from the "Sources of energy" diagram to work out which word or phrase in *italics* fits best in each gap.

a. A ________________ is a food that is useful to someone competing in a high-energy sport.

meat pie   *cream bun*   *bread roll*

b. A gymnast would benefit from eating ________________.

ice cream   *hamburgers*   *lean meat*

c. Food that is high in energy (kilojoules) suits ________________.

athletes   *sick people*   *elderly people*

d. The healthiest choice is to drink mostly ________________.

fruit juice   *milk*   *water*   *fizzy drink*

e. The nutrient that exists in the highest level in processed foods is ________________.

carbohydrate   *fat*   *protein*

f. For energy that lasts through the whole day, we should eat ________________ at every meal.

carbohydrate   *fat*   *protein*

2. Show how to balance fuel and energy by choosing the best word for each gap.

a. If you have slept well but you are still feeling tired, you should get more ________________.

food   *sleep*   *exercise*

b. If you are feeling energetic, you should get more ________________.

food   *sleep*   *exercise*

c. If you have eaten well but you are still feeling tired, you should get more ________________.

food   *sleep*   *exercise*

Snack smart

As a young person, you need to snack because your stomach is smaller than an adult's and so you run out of energy more quickly. At the same time, it's important that your snacks are nutritious and fairly low in fat and sugar.

1. Choose five healthy snacks. Each snack should come from two food groups (eg, celery and cheese, carrots and raisins). Jot down your ideas in the hand. (For some ideas, check your examples in the handout "Introducing the five food groups".)

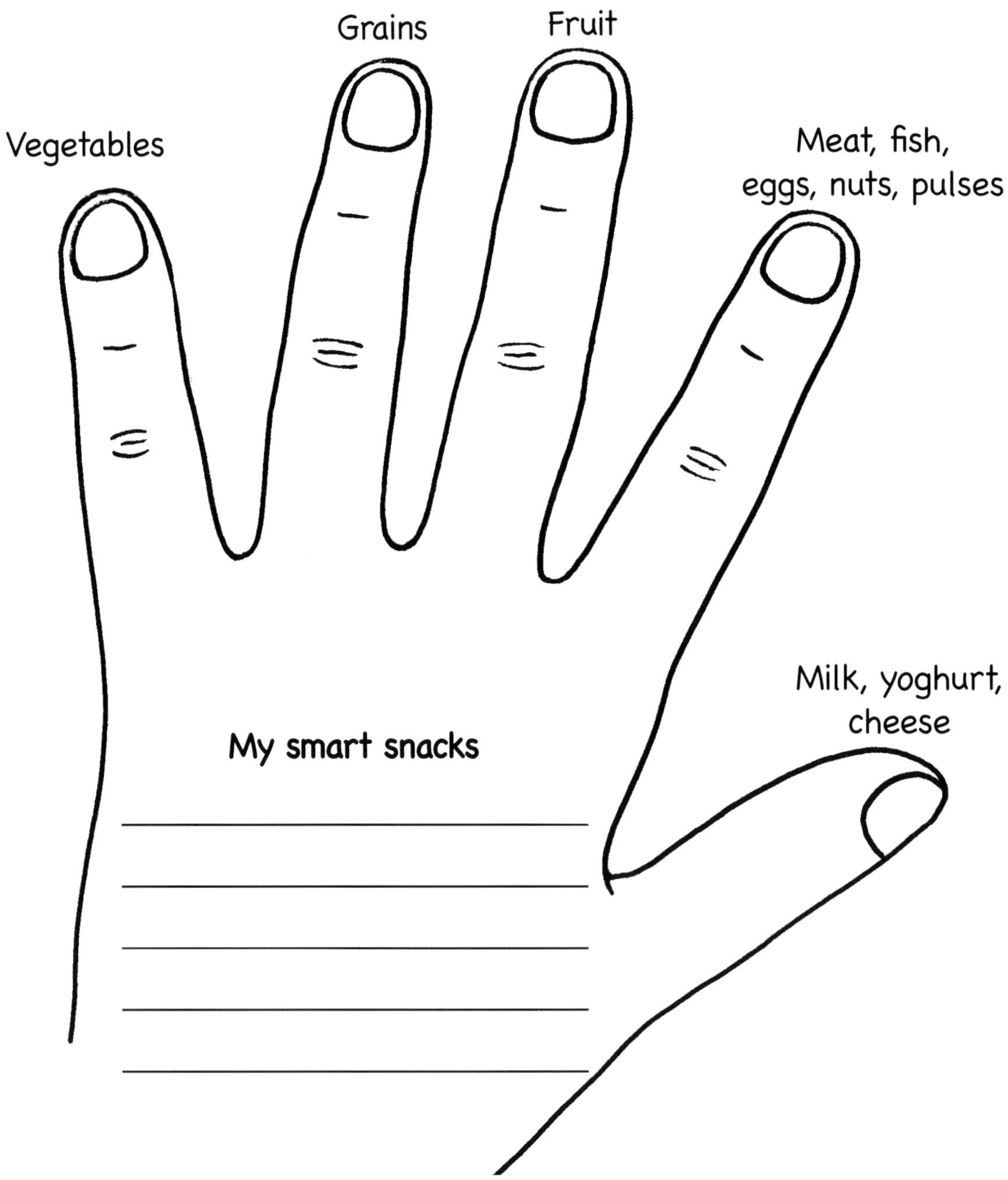

2. Now use the ideas from the hand to plan a week of healthy snacks in the chart below. You can add any other ideas you have for a healthy snack that combines two food groups. Take home the chart so that you can use it in real life!

One week of healthy snacks: my plan

	Morning snack	Afternoon snack
Monday		
Tuesday		
Wednesday		
Thursday		
Friday		

Yum … try this

Pepper boat

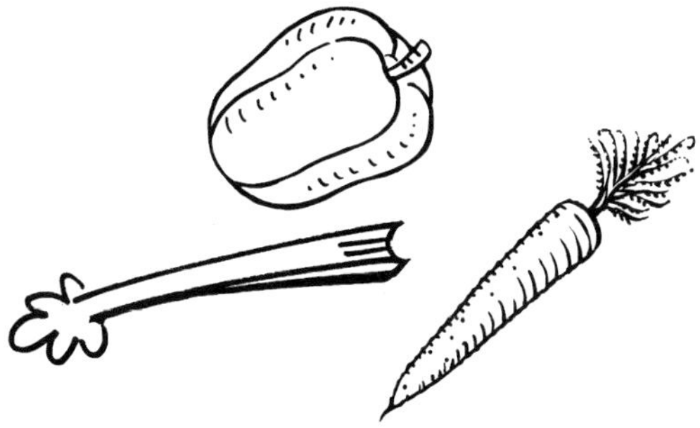

1 red, yellow or orange pepper

1 stick celery

1 carrot

Cut the pepper in half and remove seeds. Slice one half of the pepper and all of the other vegetables into thin strips. The other half of the pepper is your "boat": put a little salad dressing, mayonnaise or hummus in the bottom of it. Then place the vegetable sticks (oars) in the boat. Wrap your boat in plastic wrap – now you have a fun snack for school for yourself or a younger brother or sister.

Light lunch

Light means a food is low in fat and contains very little sugar. To get more of these healthy kinds of food, look out for "light" on food packaging.

Pies and fish and chips taste good and are okay now and then … but **not** every day! Why? Because they are high in fat. Too much fat leads to obesity (when a person is very overweight) and ill health, such as diabetes and heart problems even in young people.

1. Here are some light foods that you can enjoy for lunch. Tick ✓ the boxes to show the ones that you know and love already, and the ones that you'd like to go on a new food adventure with.

Light lunch adventure checklist

Food	I love it	I have never tried it	I would like to try it
Whole grain bread sandwiches			
Pita bread			
Wholemeal rolls			
Fillings			
cream cheese, celery, sultanas			
grated carrot, cheese, chicken			
ham, cheese and pineapple			
peanut butter and jam			
cheese and onion			
lettuce and tomato			
egg and lettuce			
Bread roll and banana (don't peel the banana until just before you eat it or it will go brown)			
Chicken drumstick			
Fruit			
Drinks			
water			
milk (in a Thermos flask)			
flavoured milk			

2. Use the ideas from the "Light lunch adventure checklist" to plan some interesting lunches for a week in the school holidays – including some you've never tried before. Take your menu plan home and ask Mum or Dad to help you make your lunch for a week. Add your own healthy ideas.

One week of light lunch adventures: my menu

Monday	
Tuesday	
Wednesday	
Thursday	
Friday	

Food goals

The "Number of servings from the five food groups" chart (on the next page) shows your goals for a healthy eating day – that is, how many servings of each food group you should aim to have each day. To complete the chart:

- write down how many servings of each food group you had yesterday
- write down some new foods from each group that you will try tomorrow ("new food day")
- later, record the number of servings you have on new food day.

Number of servings from the five food groups: my old habits and future plans

Food group	Goal: number of servings each day	How much is a serving?	Number of servings I ate yesterday	I will try these tomorrow (new food day)	Number of servings I ate on new food day (record later)
Grains	*4–6 servings*	2 slices of bread 1 bread roll 150 g cooked rice, pasta or noodles *Note: Whole grains should make up half these totals.*			
Vegetables	*4–5 servings*	150 g cooked vegetables 150 g salad			
Fruits	*1–2 servings*	1 medium apple, orange etc 2 small plums, apricots etc 4 dried apricots 1 tablespoon raisins or sultanas			
Milk	*3 servings*	250 ml low fat milk or soy milk 2 slices cheese 1 small carton yoghurt			
Eggs, meat, fish, nuts, pulses	*1–1½ servings*	2 eggs 1 drumstick 2 slices meat 1 piece fish 1 tablespoon peanut butter			
Extra foods	*1–2 servings*	1 slice cake 1 doughnut 1 can soft drink 12 chips 1½ scoops ice cream 1 small sausage roll			

Three-day food watch

1. Take this checklist home and fill in the number of servings you eat every day for three days. Use the "Number of servings from the five food groups" chart to work out how much a serving is.

My healthy diet checklist

How many servings?	Vegetables	Fruit	Bread, pasta, etc	Milk, yoghurt, etc	Meat, fish, eggs, nuts, pulses	Water	Snacks
Target: *Recommended number of servings*	*4–5*	*2*	*4–6*	*3*	*1–2*	*6*	*1–2*
Day 1							
Day 2							
Day 3							

2. Compare your eating with the recommended number of servings. How did you do? Did you meet your target for the number of servings? Yes / No

I need to eat more ______________________________.

I need to eat less ______________________________.

3. When you were filling in the checklist, did you change your eating habits to try to meet the target? Yes / No

If yes, what did you think of the change?

____

____

C. RESEARCH PROJECT: "FOOD AND WHAT'S IN IT FOR ME"

Overview and checklist

Now you will do a major research project on healthy eating and healthy lifestyles.

1. Do some research so that you can answer the questions on these handouts. See the chart below for some useful websites to get you started.

Helpful websites

kidshealth.org/kid	KidsHealth – see especially the Kids' Nutrition and Fitness Centre
www.nutritionaustralia.org	Nutrition Australia – with information on healthy lifestyles for all ages
www.5aday.com	5 A Day, The Color Way (Produce for Better Health Foundation) – information on eating fruit and vegetables by colour
www.thefruitpages.com	The Fruit Pages – everything you want to know about fruit
www.5aday.nhs.uk	UK National Health Service – tips for eating more fruit and vegetables
www.familiesonlinemagazine.com/schoollunchtips.html	School Lunch Tips (Families Online Magazine) – some healthy, fun ideas for what to eat for lunch and how to pack it

2. Staple the handouts together to make a booklet. Your booklet should also include:

- an attractive title page (including your name, title of project and due date)
- a contents page listing the names of the main sections and their page numbers
- a list of sources (websites, books, magazine articles etc) you have used for this project.

3. Tick off the checklist below as you complete each component of this research project.

Research project checklist: what I must complete

Component	Done
Title page	☐
Contents page	☐
Carbohydrates, protein, vitamins and minerals	☐
Grains: fibre and carbohydrate	☐
Vegetables: vitamins and minerals	☐
Fruit: vitamins and minerals	☐
Foods from animals: protein	☐
Drinks: what is best?	☐
Everyone is different	☐
Food labels	☐
Cereal detectives	☐
Colour your plate	☐
Ad appeal	☐
Food choice survey	☐
Summary of what I have learned	☐
List of sources used for this project	☐

Before you begin

Complete this sentence.

By the time I have finished this research project, I would like to have learned ____

____.

Carbohydrates, protein, vitamins and minerals

1. **Carbohydrates** supply us with ____________________.

   They can be found in these food groups: ____________________,

   ____________________, ____________________ and

   ____________________.

   These foods are rich in carbohydrates *(four examples)*:

   a. ____________________ c. ____________________

   b. ____________________ d. ____________________

2. **Proteins** are very important because they help to ____________________

   ____.

   They are found especially in these foods *(four examples)*:

   a. ____________________ c. ____________________

   b. ____________________ d. ____________________

3. We need **vitamins** for our health because they ____________________

   ____

   ____

   They are found especially in these foods *(six examples)*:

   a. ____________________ d. ____________________

   b. ____________________ e. ____________________

   c. ____________________ f. ____________________

4. Our bodies need small amounts of **minerals** to be healthy.

   a. The most common mineral in our body is **calcium**. It is found mostly in our ____________________. The food group that contains a lot of calcium is ____________________.

   b. Another important mineral in our body is **iron**. We get iron from animal foods such as ____________________ and plant foods such as ____________________.

Grains: fibre and carbohydrates

1. Grains are the seeds that come from the ______________ family.

Some different kinds of grain are *(four examples)*:

a. ______________________ c. ______________________

b. ______________________ d. ______________________

2. *(Refined / Whole grains)* are the best grains to eat because

____.

3. Grains should be eaten ________________________________

(rarely / sometimes / every day) because they are very high in the nutrient ______________________ which gives us the ______________________ to work and play.

4. Bran is the ____________________ part of the grain. It gives us fibre, which helps ______________________________________

____________________________.

5. Some foods that are made from grains are *(four examples)*:

a. ______________________ c. ______________________

b. ______________________ d. ______________________

6. **Bread** is mostly made from ________________________.

White bread is made from ________________________.

Whole grain bread is made from flour that has ______________

____________________________.

7. **Wheat** is a very common grain for eating in these countries *(two examples)*:

a. ______________________ b. ______________________

8. **Rice** is a very common grain for growing and eating in these countries *(two examples)*:

a. ______________________ b. ______________________

Vegetables: vitamins and minerals

Vitamins and minerals are very important for our bodies to grow strong and healthy. We can get most of the vitamins and minerals we need from plant food.

1. Vegetables come from many different parts of plants. Find two examples of vegetables that come from each part and write them in the chart below.

Plant parts we use as vegetables: some examples

Plant part	Example 1	Example 2
Leaf		
Root		
Flower		
Tuber		
Stem		
Shoot		

2. These vegetables are high in **vitamin C** *(four examples)*:

a. __________ c. __________

b. __________ d. __________

3. These vegetables are high in **vitamin A** *(four examples)*:

a. __________ c. __________

b. __________ d. __________

4. These vegetables are good to eat **raw** *(four examples)*:

a. __________ c. __________

b. __________ d. __________

5. These vegetables are delicious as **juice** *(two examples)*:

__________ __________

6. **Pulses** are special vegetables that are high in protein and iron. Two examples are:

a. __________ b. __________

Fruit: vitamins and minerals

Fruit is a good source of vitamins and carbohydrates, sugars and fibre. You should eat at least two serves of fruit per day.

1. These fruits are high in **vitamin C** *(four examples)*:

a. ______________________ c. ______________________

b. ______________________ d. ______________________

2. These fruits are high in **vitamin A** *(four examples)*:

a. ______________________ c. ______________________

b. ______________________ d. ______________________

3. An important fact about the colour of fruits is that ______________

____.

4. Fruits that are high in vitamin A and/or vitamin C can help prevent certain kinds of ____________________.

5. Fruits also contain **antioxidants**, which fight free radicals in our bodies. Free radicals can cause ______________________.

6. A fruit that is high in vitamin C is the ______________________.

7. Find (or make up) a recipe for a delicious fruit smoothie. Write it here. If you can make it as well, write a report on how it tasted.

Recipe name: ______________________________________

Ingredients: ______________________________________

Method: ____

____

Report on results: _________________________________

Extra for experts

Find out about **free radicals** and **antioxidants**, and summarise your discoveries on the back of this sheet. Concentrate on the information that is most relevant to healthy lifestyles.

Foods from animals: protein

Protein is important for a healthy body. Animals and some vegetables give us protein.

1. Complete this chart, which lists farm animals (on the left) and the meat that is made from them (on the right). Give six examples (eg, pig–pork).

Meat that comes from animals: some examples

Animal	Meat

2. Protein is necessary for building ______________________________

____

3. Eggs are another animal food high in protein. Eggs contain other useful nutrients such as ______________________________.

4. These vegetables also give us protein *(two examples)*:

a. ____________________ b. ____________________

5. You would get enough protein by eating these four foods each day:

a. ____________________ c. ____________________

b. ____________________ d. ____________________

6. Protein is important but we have to be careful not to eat too much of it because ______________________________.

Drinks: what is best?

1. The best drink is ______________ because ______________________

____.

2. We need to drink ____________ glasses of this best drink every day.

3. Milk is also an excellent drink because ________________________

____.

4. People who are allergic to cow's milk can drink __________________

instead as a good source of calcium.

5. Fruit drinks have more sugar and more kilojoules than most soft drinks. True / False

6. A good nutrient in fruit drink is __________________.

7. I found out that this soft drink, ____________________ has ____

teaspoons or ____ grams of sugar in each can.

8. In the chart below, give two examples of fruit drinks and two examples of soft drinks and list the sugar content of each one.

Sugar in drinks: my findings

	Amount of sugar per 100 grams	
	Fruit drink	Soft drink
Example 1	Name: __________________ Sugar: __________ per 100 g	Name: __________________ Sugar: __________ per 100 g
Example 2	Name: __________________ Sugar: __________ per 100 g	Name: __________________ Sugar: __________ per 100 g

9. The sugar in fruit drinks and soft drinks causes __________________

____.

Everyone is different

So far you have been researching some general advice about healthy eating. Now you will look at some people who do not follow all of this advice but who can still eat in healthy ways.

You may find these websites helpful:

http://www.fankids.org/FANKid/kidindex.html Food Allergy News for Kids

http://www.goveg.com GoVeg.com

1. Some people do not eat certain foods because they have a **food allergy**.

a. What is a food allergy? ____________________

____

b. What is the most common food allergy? ____________________

c. Give two other examples of common food allergies.

____________________ ____________________

2. Some people do not eat meat or fish because they are **vegetarians**.

a. What are three reasons why a person may become a vegetarian? ____________________

____________________ ____________________

b. What advice would you give to a vegetarian so that they eat a healthy diet without meat or fish?

____

____

3. Some people do not eat certain foods because of their **religion**. Choose one of the religions listed below and find out more about what foods that people who follow this religion eat and do not eat.

Islam *Hinduism* *Judaism* *Buddhism*

Religion: ____________________

Report on diet: ____________________

____

____

____

Food labels

A food label tells you which nutrients are in a food. It also tells you how much of each nutrient is in a food, in terms of the amount in each serve or the amount in 100 grams of the food. The "per 100 g" information is more precise.

1. Investigate these foods to find out how much **sugar**, **sodium** and **saturated fat per 100 g** is in each one. Then use this information to answer the questions under the chart.

Sugar, sodium and saturated fat in foods: my findings

Food	Sugar level per 100 g	Sodium level per 100 g	Saturated fat level per 100 g
These levels are OK (< means "less than")	< 27 g	< 600 mg	< 20 g
Sausages			
Ham			
Canned salmon			
Baked beans			
Muesli bar			
Full milk			
Low fat milk			
Fish fingers			
Meat pie			
Crisps			

2. Which food in the chart is highest in sugar? ____________________

3. Which food is highest in sodium? ____________________

4. Which food is highest in saturated fat? ____________________

5. Which food is highest in all three ingredients? ____________________

6. One thing I have learned from filling out this chart is ____________

____

Cereal detectives

Many people think of breakfast cereals as a healthy food … but many of these cereals may not be as healthy as we thought. Researchers have found that many popular breakfast cereals contain more than 30% sugar and are more salty than crisps.

1. Investigate six popular brands of cereal sold in a supermarket near you. In the chart below, record the sugar and sodium (salt) levels for each one (more than 27 g of sugar per 100 g or more than 600 g of salt per 100 g is too high).

Sugar and sodium in cereals: my findings from a supermarket investigation

Cereal	Sugar per 100 g	Sodium per 100 g
These levels are OK (< means "less than")	< 27 g	< 600 mg

2. Look at the cereals you have at home. Record their sugar and sodium levels in the chart below.

Sugar and sodium in cereals: my findings from my home investigations

Our cereal	Sugar per 100 g	Sodium per 100 g

3. Find out which three cereals in your local supermarket are the **healthiest** (in terms of having the lowest sugar and sodium levels) and which three are **least healthy** (ie, with the highest sugar and sodium levels). Record your findings in the charts below.

The top three cereals: my findings

Healthy cereal	Sugar per 100 g	Sodium per 100 g

Cereal offenders – too much sugar or too much salt: my findings

Unhealthy cereal	Sugar per 100 g	Sodium per 100 g

4. Why do you think some cereals contain so much sugar and/or sodium? ______________________________

____

____

Colour your plate

Research shows that colourful vegetables and fruit provide the essential vitamins, minerals and fibre that your body needs. Try to eat natural foods from every colour of the spectrum (5–9 servings in total).

1. These are the colours of the spectrum:

a. ______________________ e. ______________________

b. ______________________ f. ______________________

c. ______________________ g. ______________________

d. ______________________

2. List three fruits for each colour of the spectrum shown in the chart.

The fruit rainbow: some examples

	Colour			
Example	Red	Orange or yellow	Green	Blue or purple
1				
2				
3				

3. List three vegetables for each colour shown in the chart.

The vegetable rainbow: some examples

	Colour				
Example	Red	Orange or yellow	Green	Blue or purple	White
1					
2					
3					

Ad appeal

TV, radio and magazine advertisements try to make particular products appealing so that we will buy them. Investigate some TV advertisements for five different foods. What "ad appeal" strategies do they use to try to get you to buy the food? Who are they targeting? Write your findings in the chart below. One example is given to get you started.

TV advertisements for food: my findings

Food item advertised	Strategy for ad appeal	Target buyers
Meal package at Fried Takeaways	You get a free toy with every meal.	Kids who collect toys

Choosing foods: a survey

1. Survey your family and friends to find out which criterion (or way of judging) they use most to help them choose food. Then use this information to answer the questions below.

Food choice survey

Name	When you are deciding whether to buy a food, which one of these criteria do you consider most of all? (Tick the answer.)					
	Appearance	Taste	Nutrition	Convenience	Familiarity	Cost
Total						

2. The most common view is that ________________ is the most important criterion.

3. The most common view is that ________________ is the least important criterion.

4. I agree / disagree with the most common view because

____

____

5. I would rank the six criteria above in this order, from most important to least important:

____

____

Summary of what I have learned

Look back at the data you have collected for this research project. Summarise (in bullet points) the key information about healthy eating and healthy living that you have learned.

- ____
- ____
- ____
- ____
- ____
- ____
- ____
- ____

Here are some other interesting facts that I learned during my research:

____

____

____

____

____

Here are some questions that came up during my research and that I would now like to find out the answer to:

____

____

____

____

____

____

D. ACTIVE KIDS ARE HEALTHY KIDS

Active kid questionnaire

1. Are you active? Yes / No

2. Tick the activities you like to do.

- ☐ Ride a bike
- ☐ Watch TV
- ☐ Play cricket
- ☐ Go skateboarding
- ☐ Dance
- ☐ Play tennis
- ☐ Swim
- ☐ Read books
- ☐ Do karate
- ☐ Play basketball
- ☐ Do athletics
- ☐ Play on PlayStation
- ☐ Play netball
- ☐ Play football
- ☐ Go on trampoline
- ☐ Play computer games

3. Cross out the four activities on the list that are not active.

4. There are 12 "active" activities on the list. How many of them do you like doing? ______________

5. What is an important reason why a child may not be able to do any of the "active" activities on the list? ______________________

____

6. Write down four more active things you like to do.

a. ______________________ c. ______________________

b. ______________________ d. ______________________

Aim for 1 hour of active play every day.

Get UP and GO Spaceship

Colour the spaceship. Hang the poster in your bedroom.

Do less

Watching TV,
playing computer games,
sitting around and eating

Do more

(2–3 times a week)
Playing outside – skipping, dancing,
karate, swinging, climbing

Do more and more

(3–5 times a week)
Biking, rollerblading, swimming, skateboarding,
football, netball, tennis, running

Do lots of (every day)

Playing outside, walking the dog, walking to the shop, walking to school, picking up your toys, doing chores, running about, playing in the playground, walking up and down stairs, jumping on the trampoline, playing on a scooter, going for a walk

Be active, be healthy!

Exercise goals

Aim to exercise for at least one hour every day (more is better). When you are counting up your active hours, include PE, sport, playtime, lunchtime and all your time out of school (after school and the weekend).

1. Fill in the "My active goals" chart to show your goals for exercise over one week. For each day, pick four activities from the Get UP and GO Spaceship that you will aim to do.

My active goals

	15 minutes, 4 times a day			
	Activity 1	Activity 2	Activity 3	Activity 4
Mon				
Tues				
Wed				
Thurs				
Fri				
Sat				
Sun				

2. Hang "My active goals" on the fridge at home. Tick ⌚ each activity as you do it. After a week, bring this goal sheet back to school and tell your class about what you did.

E. HOW MUCH DO YOU KNOW?

Teacher note: Answers to these games are given at the end of this section.

Healthy living quiz

1. What colours of vegetables and fruit should you eat every day?

____

2. How many hours of sleep do 5- to 12-year-olds need? __________

3. Name two different foods in the grains group.

a. ____________________ b. ____________________

4. How much exercise should 10- to 12-year-olds do each day?

____

5. Name the five major food groups.

a. ____________________ d. ____________________

b. ____________________ e. ____________________

c. ____________________

6. What food groups are in the main part of the Healthy Living Spaceship?

____

____

7. What food group is our main source of calcium? ____________

8. What foods are our main source of vitamins and minerals?

____

9. Name two foods that are good sources of protein.

a. ____________________ b. ____________________

10. Carbohydrates give our bodies ____________________.

Healthy eating crossword puzzle

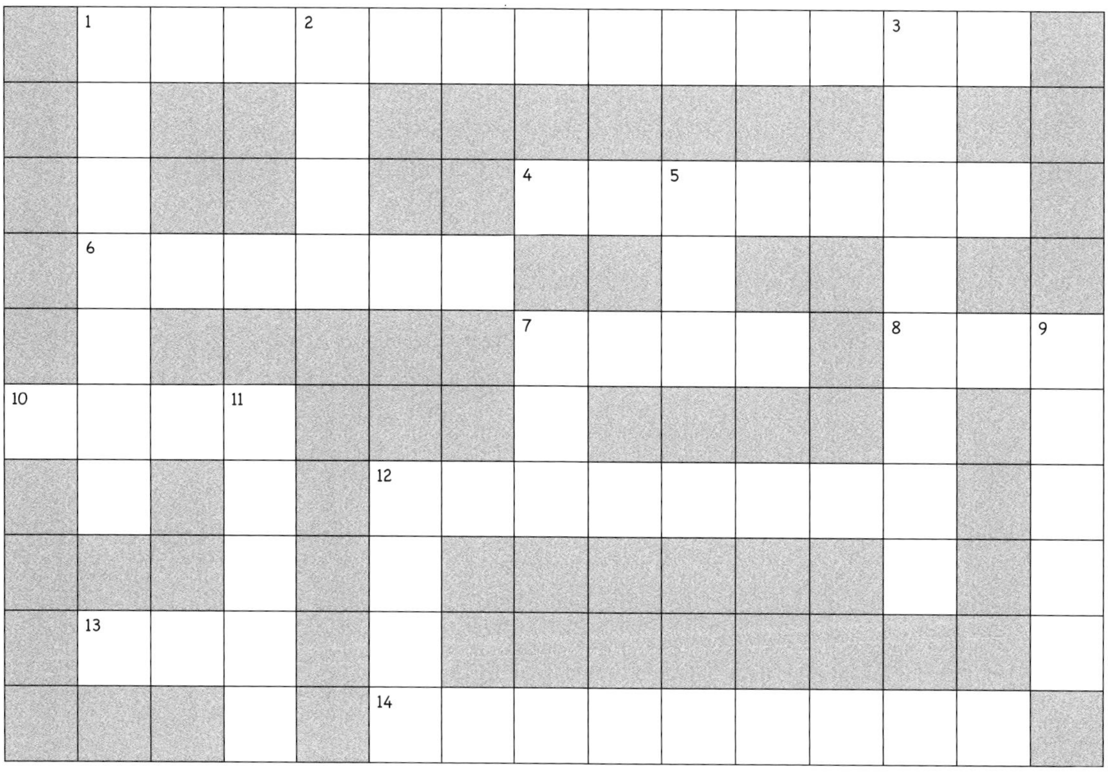

Across

1. Energy foods are high in these
4. Common grain food in many Asian countries
6. Breakfast food
7. An easy form of exercise
8. We get milk from this animal
10. These foods give us protein
12. Vital nutrient found in fruit and vegetables
13. A whole grain
14. Energy measure

Down

1. Teeth and bones need it
2. One colour of the spectrum to eat
3. Do it every day for good health
5. You need it but only in small amounts
7. Fit kids might do this in a race
9. Drink lots of this
11. 5- to 12-year-olds need 10–11 hours of this every day
12. Drink 1 glass of this every day

Jumbled nutrition

Unjumble the letters to make a *Healthy Eating, Healthy Living* word.

1. guhtryo ____________

2. shecee ____________

3. gtebelasve ____________

4. lusspe ____________

5. bifer ____________

6. aaspt ____________

7. typuolr ____________

8. cborcoil ____________

Great game challenge

Here's your chance to help make it fun to be active.

Your mission

Make up a game in which players must be active most of the time. Your game should have:

- a clear goal or purpose
- clear rules (but not too many – make sure every rule helps to play the game)
- a variety of activities (eg, skipping, running forwards, running backwards, throwing a ball)
- one or more items of sports equipment (eg, ball, racquet, mini-trampoline).

Jot down your ideas on the back of this sheet then write a good copy in which you explain your game (with diagrams if that helps).

Your test

Try out how your game works in practice.

First, go through the game with your partner to try to identify any problems, and fix them (eg, by changing a rule or changing an activity). You might think of ways to make it even better, too.

Next, get a group together to play your game. Make sure everyone is clear about what to do before the game begins.

Your reflections

Write a brief report on how the game went. What worked well, and what might you change for next time?

____

____

Your next challenge

Create a game for children who have some kind of physical disability. You can decide on what kind or kinds of disability you are designing the game around. What's important is that you try to provide them with a variety of "active" activities that they can do.

You may be able to adapt your first game for this new game, or you may create an entirely new game.

Answers

Answers to healthy living quiz

1. All the colours of the spectrum or red, orange, yellow, green, blue (indigo, violet)
2. 10–11 hours
3. Your answer should be any two of: bread, pasta, rice, noodles, cereals.
4. At least one hour
5. a. Vegetables
   b. Fruit
   c. Dairy foods – milk, yoghurt, cheese
   d. Meat, fish, eggs, nuts, pulses
   e. Grains – bread, cereals, pasta, rice, noodles
6. Vegetables, fruit, grains
7. Dairy – milk, cheese, yoghurt
8. Fruit and vegetables
9. Your answer should be any two of: nuts, meat, fish, eggs, pulses
10. Energy

Answers to healthy eating crossword puzzle

	[1]C	A	R	[2]B	O	H	Y	D	R	A	T	[3]E	S	
	A			L								X		
	L			U			[4]N	O	[5]O	D	L	E	S	
	[6]C	E	R	E	A	L			I			R		
	I						[7]W	A	L	K		[8]C	O	[9]W
[10]N	U	T	[11]S				I					I		A
	M		L		[12]M	I	N	E	R	A	L	S		T
			E		I							E		E
	[13]R	Y	E		L									R
			P		[14]K	I	L	O	J	O	U	L	E	

Answers to jumbled nutrition

1. yoghurt
2. cheese
3. vegetables
4. pulses
5. fibre
6. pasta
7. poultry
8. broccoli

FURTHER RESOURCES: HEALTHY EATING WEBSITES

Note: These website addresses were correct at the time of publication. If you cannot find one or more of these sites, use some of the other details given to locate them through a search engine.

The websites are provided by the author as optional resources that may be of use to the teacher. Essential Resources takes no responsibility for their content.

British Heart Foundation. <www.bhf.org.uk>. *Includes games and information on a healthy lifestyle.*

Centers for Disease Control and Prevention (USA). BAM! Body and mind. <www.bam.gov/index.html>. *Accessible nutritional and other health information for children.*

DirectgovKids (UK). <www.directgovkids.co.uk>. *Visit the supermarket and the school for nutrition-related activities.*

Fresh for Kids. <www.freshforkids.com.au>. *Australian-based information on healthy lifestyles, designed to appeal to children.*

Health Insite (Australia). Healthy lunch boxes. <www.healthinsite.gov.au/topics/Healthy_Lunch_Boxes>. *Links to resources on healthy lunches and other food for children.*

Healthy Choices for Kids Online (USA). <www.healthychoices.org>. *Information can be photocopied for educational purposes.*

KidsHealth (USA). <kidshealth.org>. *Wide-ranging information that includes a Kids' Nutrition and Fitness Centre.*

LearntobeHealthy (USA). <www.learntobehealthy.org>. *Free activites and lesson plans.*

National Health Service (UK). *Top tips for eating more fruit and veg.* <www.5aday.nhs.uk>. *Practical ideas for healthy eating.*

National Institutes of Health, National Institute of Child Health and Human Development (USA). Milk matters. <www.nichd.nih.gov/milk/prob/calcium_need.cfm>. *Calcium educational campaign, including material designed for children.*

Nestlé Australia. <www.nestle.com.au>. *Nutritional information at each major stage of the life cycle and tools such as BMI and nutrient calculators.*

Nutrition Australia. <www.nutritionaustralia.org>. *Australian-based nutritional information, with a scientific emphasis, from a non-government organisation.*

PediatricObesity (USA). Helping parents raise healthy children. <www.pediatricobesity.com>. *Lifestyle news and advice aimed particularly at parents.*

Produce for Better Health Foundation (USA). 5 A Day, The Color Way. <www.5aday.com >. *Information for both pupils and educators on eating fruit and vegetables by colour.*